# My Bible Values

This book belongs to:

# 52 Value topics

- Diligence ........................................................................................... 4
- Obedience ........................................................................................ 5
- Self-control ...................................................................................... 6
- Humility ............................................................................................ 7
- Initiative .......................................................................................... 8
- Honesty ........................................................................................... 9
- Patience ......................................................................................... 10
- Encouragement ............................................................................... 11
- Comparing ...................................................................................... 12
- Confidence ..................................................................................... 13
- Responsibility ................................................................................. 14
- Follow rules .................................................................................... 15
- Willingness ..................................................................................... 16
- Gratitude ........................................................................................ 17
- Understanding ................................................................................ 18
- Decisions ........................................................................................ 19
- Faithfulness ................................................................................... 20
- Unselfishness ................................................................................. 21
- Attentiveness ................................................................................. 22
- Caring ............................................................................................. 23
- Courage .......................................................................................... 24
- Devotion ......................................................................................... 25
- Wisdom ........................................................................................... 26
- Appreciation ................................................................................... 27
- Endurance ...................................................................................... 28

| | |
|---|---|
| Service | 29 |
| Determination | 30 |
| Teamwork | 31 |
| Conviction | 32 |
| Hopefulness | 33 |
| Perseverance | 34 |
| Beauty | 35 |
| Availability | 36 |
| Take action | 37 |
| Boldness | 38 |
| Kindness | 39 |
| Cheerfulness | 40 |
| Peer-Pressure | 41 |
| Gentleness | 42 |
| Hospitality | 43 |
| Friendship | 44 |
| Forgiveness | 45 |
| Flexibility | 46 |
| Sharing | 47 |
| Thankfulness | 48 |
| I'm sorry | 49 |
| Enthusiasm | 50 |
| Concentration | 51 |
| Equality | 52 |
| Dependable | 53 |
| Fairness | 54 |
| Self-esteem | 55 |
| Respect | 56 |

# Diligence

Diligence is to do a good job, and to continue until it's done.

Yay! I was careful and thorough, and I even had fun!

**Diligent hands that work hard make you rich.**
(Proverbs 10:4)

# Obedience

Obedience is to do the things that are good and right.

To do as I am told even when there is no one in sight.

Do what is right and good in God's sight.
(Deuteronomy 6:18)

# Humility

I accept that I'm not good enough on my own; some help I need.

God is all mighty and powerful. With His help I can succeed.

God goes against the proud, but gives grace to the humble.
(James 4:6)

# Initiative

I do things that need to be done even before being asked.

I am quick to look for opportunities to help others in their tasks.

Be rich in doing good deeds. Be happy to give and ready to share.
(1 Timothy 6:18)

# Honesty

I say and do things that are true and right.

Being trustworthy is pleasing in God's sight.

The Lord is pleased with those who tell the truth.
(Proverbs 12:22b)

# Patience

Patience is waiting for things when I want them right away.

It's staying positive, and trusting that everything is going to be okay.

Be strong in heart and wait patiently for God.
(Psalm 27:14)

# Encouragement

God comforts and helps me feel better when I am sad.

With a kind word or a loving deed I can help others feel glad.

Patience and encouragement come from God.
(Romans 15:5)

# Willingness

I do things that need to be done when I am asked.

I might not understand why, but I will still do the task.

If you are willing and obedient, you will be blessed.
(Isaiah 1:19)

# Gratitude

I give honor and praise to God for caring for me.

Everyone appreciates gratitude, don't you agree?

Come to God with thanksgiving and praise.
(Psalm 100:4)

# Understanding

I understand that you are feeling sad.
I'll help and do what I can to make you feel glad.

God is merciful and gracious, full of love and faithfulness.
(Psalm 86:15)

# Decisions

God can help me choose to do what is right.

When I follow His advice, things turn out alright.

If you don't know what to do, ask for God's help.
(James 1:5)

# Unselfishness

I put the needs of others above my own,
I give and share even if little I own.

Don't just look out for yourself,
but think about the good of others.
(Philippians 2:4)

# Caring

God's love and kindness is the best care,

Whenever we need Him, He's always there.

**Whenever possible, do good to people who need help.**
(Proverbs 3:27)

# Courage

When I'm faced with problems and fear comes my way,

I stand strong and brave, with God's help I won't sway.

Be strong and of good courage.
Don't be afraid; because God will go with you.
(Deuteronomy 31:6)

# Endurance

I persevere till the very end.

I don't give up and quit. On God I depend.

You must hold on, so you can do what God wants and receive what he has promised.

(Hebrews 10:36)

# Service

When I see someone in need, I stop to help out.

It may be small, but it's one way I can serve, no doubt.

Whatever you do, work as though you are doing it for the Lord.
(Colossians 3:23)

# Determination

I work hard to finish what I start. I don't just do a little part.

I see it through to the end. Now that is being smart.

Keep your eyes focused on what is right.
Look straight ahead to what is good.
(Proverbs 4:25)

# Hopefulness

Scared, freaked out, I was worried as can be.

But not for long, because Jesus calmed me.

Your hope is in God's promises, like an anchor, firm and secure.
(Hebrews 6:18-19)

# Perseverance

I keep on working hard without giving in.

Even when it gets tough, I do my best to win.

We will receive the reward for our work at just the right time, if we don't give up.
(Galatians 6:9b)

# Beauty

Beauty is not just about the things that I wear,

With God in me, His love shines everywhere.

True beauty comes from inside you.
It is the beauty of a gentle and quiet spirit.
(1 Peter 3:3,4)

# Take action

I act quickly when someone needs a helping hand,
And do what I can even if it's not what I'd planned.

Let us love, not only in word or talk, but in deed and in truth.
(1 John 3:18)

# Boldness

I am brave when I speak to others about God.

I show courage whether they boo or they applaud.

May you speak the Word of God with boldness.
(Acts 4:29)

# Cheerfulness

A joyful heart makes a cheerful face.
(Proverbs 15:13)

# Gentleness

Little brother is sick and needs to rest.

"Wipe your nose softly." I suggest.

I put a pillow under his head.

And I'll be real quiet while he's in bed.

Come and learn from me, for I am meek and gentle in heart.
(Matthew 11:28-29)

# Hospitality

I say "Welcome!" to visitors at the door.
I take their coat, offer a seat and more.
Now they're comfortable and cared for,
Being hospitable is never a bore.

**Welcome others into your homes without complaining.**
(1 Peter 4:9)

# Friendship

A true friend will help even when it's difficult to do.

I'm there through the good and the bad, when I'm a friend to you.

A man that has friends must show himself friendly.

(Proverbs 18:24)

# Sharing

I'll see the needs of others and share what I can.

I'll do this with a willing heart; that's God's plan.

Be generous and ready to share with others.
(1 Timothy 6:18)

# Thankfulness

Look at all the great things God has done. Let's remember to thank Him for each one.

Give thanks in all things, for this is pleasing to God.
(I Thessal onians 5:18)

# Concentration

Stop, wait, look and go.

Red light, green light. Whoa!

It takes all of my attention,

To move in the right direction.

God gives us a spirit of power, love and self-control.
(2 Timothy 1:7)

# Dependable

Did you fall down while on your way?
I'll get help right away.
You can trust me, I'll do as I say.
You can rely on me any day.

When you keep your word, God's love is seen in you.
1 John 2:6

# Fairness

The rules are there to say, "Let's be fair when we play".

Whether I loose or I win, I will take it with a grin.

God rules the nations with fairness.
(Psalm 9:8)

# Self-esteem

I've got a plan, to be a big man.

So I practice hanging clothes, and my confidence grows.

I give new things a go, I can do it, you know.

Don't lose your courage; it will bring you great reward.
(Hebrews 10:35)

# More books from iCharacter.org

## iCharacter

Published by iCharacter Limited ®. (Ireland)
Texts: Agnes de Bezenac.
Illustrations: Agnes de Bezenac
Quotes: Rephrased from citations and Bible verses.
Proofreading: iCharacter team and Martine Caroni
Copyright 2019 iCharacter Limited

Copyright © 2019 by iCharacter Limited ®. All rights reserved. No part of this book may be reproduced in any form or by any electronic or mechanical means, including information storage and retrieval systems, without written permission from the publisher or author, except in the case of a reviewer, who may quote brief passages embodied in critical articles or in a review.